THE PÈRE MARQUETTE
LECTURE IN THEOLOGY
1994

# SEEKING GOD
# IN
# CONTEMPORARY
# CULTURE

REMBERT G. WEAKLAND, O.S.B.

ARCHBISHOP OF MILWAUKEE

MARQUETTE UNIVERSITY PRESS
MILWAUKEE, WISCONSIN

Manufactured in the United States of America

ISBN 0-87462-549-1

# Foreword

The 1994 Père Marquette Lecture in Theology is the twenty-fifth in a series commemorating the missions and explorations of Père Jacques Marquette, S.J. (1637-75). This series of annual lectures was begun in 1969 under the auspices of the Marquette University Department of Theology.

The Joseph A. Auchter Family Endowment Fund has endowed the lecture series. Joseph Auchter (1894-1986), a native of Milwaukee, was a banking and paper industry executive and a longtime supporter of education. The fund was established by his children as a memorial to him.

We are pleased to join this silver anniversary of the Père Marquette Lecture series to the one hundred and fiftieth anniversary of the founding of the Milwaukee Archdiocese and are therefore doubly pleased to have as our lecturer

for this year the Most Reverend Rembert G.
Weakland, O.S.B., Archbishop of Milwaukee.
Archbishop Weakland was born in Patton, Pennsylvania in 1927. He began religious life as a
Benedictine novice at St. Vincent Archabbey in
Latrobe, Pennsylvania in 1945 and was sol-
emnly professed as a monk four years later at
Solesmes Abbey in France. Philosophical and
theological studies leading to ordination were
pursued at St. Vincent Seminary in Latrobe and
at the International Benedictine College of
Sant'Anselmo in Rome. He was ordained in
1951 in Italy. Thereafter Archbishop Weakland
studied music in Italy, France, Germany, and, in
the United States, at the Juilliard School of
Music and at Columbia University. Between
1957 and 1963 he taught music at St. Vincent
College, held memberships and offices in several
prominent national and international societies
and associations, lectured throughout Europe
and America, and authored several articles on
music and liturgy. He is the author of The Play
of Daniel. In 1963 Archbishop Weakland was
elected Coadjutor Archabbot of St. Vincent
Archabbey and made the Chancellor and Chair-
man of the Board of Directors of St. Vincent
College. The next year he received a papal

appointment as a consultor to the Commission for Implementing the Constitution on the Sacred Liturgy of the Second Vatican Council. He was appointed a member in 1968. In 1967 Archbishop Weakland was elected Abbot Primate of the International Benedictine Confederation and became the Chancellor of the College of Sant'Anselmo in Rome. He was reelected in 1973. During this time he participated in three Synods of Bishops. In 1977 Pope Paul VI appointed the Abbot Primate as Archbishop of Milwaukee and Metropolitan of the Province of Milwaukee. Since this appointment Archbishop Weakland has participated in the 1987 Synod of Bishops, been the past-Chairman of the National Conference of Catholic Bishops' ad hoc Committee on Catholic Social Teaching and the U.S. Economy which drafted the important Pastoral Letter on the Economy. He has been past-Chair of the NCCB Committee for Ecumenical and Interreligious Affairs and is currently Co-Chairman of this Committee's Dialogue between Roman Catholic and Eastern Orthodox Churches, a member of the Roman Catholic-Eastern Orthodox Theological Consultation and an advisor on the North American Board for East-West Dialog. In addition he has served on the NCCB Committee on the Mission and Structure of the NCCB and the Administrative Board of the United States Catholic Conference. Locally he is a member of the Board of Directors of the Wisconsin Catholic Conference and the Vice-President of the Interfaith Conference of Greater Milwaukee.

In the present lecture, given on March 27, 1994, Archbishop Weakland, drawing on his wide experience, examines some of the issues and problems relating to the contemporary search for God.

Rev. Earl Muller, S.J.

# Seeking God
# in
# Contemporary Culture

Benedict, in his Rule for Monks, gives various criteria for judging if a novice has the correct motivation. The first of these criteria reads as follows: "the concern must be whether the novice truly seeks God" (*si revera Deum quaeret,* chapter 58). It is important to note that Benedict does not say that the novice must find God, but only that the novice must be truly searching for God. In fact, it would probably be a negative sign if the novice were content that he had found God.

Benedict continues to elaborate on this search by mentioning three other factors: "whether he shows eagerness for the Work of God, for obedience and for trials (*opprobria*)."[1] The Work of God is Benedict's classic term for the Divine Office or the community prayer. The novice must be seeking God in prayer. The novice must also be taught that the search for God is full of hardships and difficulties. Thus, the realism of the vicissitudes of this life becomes also a place where God is to be found. Obedience, in Benedict's way of thinking, is a basic Christian concept, broader than that which religious later took the term to mean. It implies listening to God's voice and seeking God's will in prayer, in the Rule and tradition, in the figure of the superior. It means that the monk sees God working through others. It is sacramental in character. Searching for God is a part of the Christian life in every epoch. It is affected by the culture and the attitudes that are in vogue at the time. Each generation seeks in a different way. The search for God today as in all epochs of history is not just a theological problem; it also has important pastoral implications. Too often the cultural influences, both positive and negative, are not reflected upon, are not articulated. Pastoral ministry then operates in a vacuum.

*Overview: The God-question.*

It is not surprising to me that today teenagers ask more God-questions than Jesus-questions. The workings of God seem to be even more important to them than moral questions. Their parents are more likely to ask about ecclesial and "Churchy" issues, about changes in worship, about social concerns. Youngsters do not at once go on to ask about Jesus or even the Bible but seem to get stuck on the God-questions. They are concerned both about the existence of God and the relationship between God and what happens on this earth in the here and now. They raise up for any teacher of the faith the pastoral concern: where do people of our day and age, of our modern or post-modern culture, seek God? How have the cultural presuppositions of our day affected our concept of God and how God acts or interacts with this world? So often, these questions are passed over and more practical issues are dwelt on. The God-questions cannot be omitted if the catechesis is to be effective.

We all meet variations on the God-question daily. Some profess a belief in God, but then live as practical atheists. That is, they find no place for God in their daily lives. Faith does not influence action. Because God for them is not needed as an explanation of the world and what happens here, they ignore all aspects of religion. They are not hostile toward religion, just indifferent. What cannot be put under a microscope may be interesting but not of importance for their daily living. Others seem to find God within themselves. They place emphasis on inner emotions and experiences. Their God is a God-within. That they may share this same God with others is of no concern. Their God is also the one who takes them beyond themselves, carries them, as it were, in times of need and trouble or just permits them to make the extra "jump" shot. Their God is the God of the athletes or of Alcoholics Anonymous.

These approaches to God affect how Catholics relate to the Mass and the sacraments, to the clergy and other ministers, to the Church in general. That God could use material objects or acts (sacraments), that God could act through designated people (authority), that the Church is an instrument and not just an occasion of grace — all these concepts are colored by how the culture portrays God or the absence of God and how God's interaction with this world is conceived. If there has been a falling off, for example, among Catholics of the practice of confession, one has to ask how the general cultural milieu of our day has affected this sacrament. It is not enough just to say that there is a lack of discipline or a diminution of a sense of sin in our day among younger Catholics. There is also a change in the attitudes one has towards God.

Theologians have become much more aware of the need to look at the cultural milieu when discussing the way they pursue their science.[2] It is not enough just to cite Scripture, or talk about underpinning philosophical principles of a teaching, one must also see the cultural matrix that has and will continue to influence the believer. The constant dialectic between the tradition, on one hand, as contained in Scripture and the accumulated teaching of the Church, and the culture of the times, on the other, has become more evident in our day. Because we are in a period of cultural change and ambiguity, it is important to examine the basic relationship between searching for God and the cultural climate we live in.

An example of this kind of relationship can be seen in the divergent responses to the natural disasters that have been common in the last years: earthquakes on the West Coast, flooding in the Midwest, hurricanes in the South. Some interpreted these in the older cultural model as ways in which God is punishing us humans or at least sending us a message that would lead to conversion. One hears this interpretation, especially among those who still feel they have the right to speak in God's name and interpret God's intentions to others. That is why the more fundamentalist tradition feels freer to do so. Others shied away from such interpretations, saw the disasters as "natural" or attributable to natural causes, and then sought to find the voice of God in the kindness and loving responses of others to those placed in need by these phenomena.

This example shows that there is not one cultural matrix, neatly defined, that characterizes all of contemporary society. Nevertheless, one has seen a shift in that culture insofar as it relates to religion, so that the reactions that come out of an older cultural picture can no longer be taken as normative. Most people tend to smile when they hear such voices that seem to interpret God's mind to them. They do not, for the most part, take such assertions seriously.

In this essay I would like to try to unravel some of the strains in our culture that affect our notion of God and point out how this has affected and will continue to affect our Catholic pastoral practice.

Let me say at once that I do not believe that it is either fruitful or useful to try to create a Catholic culture that is in opposition to the general culture of our age and that provides a safe haven for believers. I do not think that one can live consciously in two cultures simultaneously. Rather, one lives in a culture, is influenced by it, and tries to influence it. One tries to absorb the best that is found there and give it direction.[3] To ignore, for example, in our day the communications explosion would be both fruitless and useless. Even those who claim to seek to live in another "Churchy" culture really do not do so and cannot avoid the power over them of the contemporary world in which they live. Sometimes it is helpful to analyze the culture and know what is being accepted and what is being rejected or modified so that it is done consciously and with reflection. For most of us, those acceptances and rejections are done on the basis of Catholic tradition and Catholic values and are at times done intuitively. The role of pastoral theology is to try to "explicitate" that which is often done by the faithful implicitly.

What follows is an attempt to do such reflection on the single issue of God and how God relates to this world and how the traditional Catholic approach has been modified over the decades by the presuppositions of modern culture — or post-modern, if you will.

## 1. The Scientific Hypothesis.

The question today is not: does God exist? But rather: what difference does it make? Proofs for the existence of God are not as important as the relevancy of God to what is happening here and now. Teenagers imply this skepticism about relevancy when they ask their God-questions. I can assure you that they have never heard of Nietzsche nor of Thomas Altizer, nor of William Hamilton. They have not heard of David Tracy nor Harvey Cox.[4]

One often calls this process of slowly eliminating God from the explanation of the universe and what is happening here as a process of "secularization." "Giving the world its due" is another way of putting it. *The Pastoral Constitution on the Church in the Modern World (Gaudium et spes)* of Vatican Council II gave also to this world its independence and intrinsic value.[5] Even though it can be proven that the ultimate results of a secularization process, namely, the creation of a culture of total unbelief, has not taken place, the process has been, nevertheless, a real one and has affected our present generation.[6] God is simply left out as explanation of what is happening in the world. I have often called this position "practical atheism." The existence of God is not denied, just its importance and relevancy to modern living. God is simply superfluous when one comes to explaining the phenomena of this world. Formerly God was often excluded from the life and consciousness of a believer because the believer was living by other values that conflicted with those of faith. Now God can be excluded simply as not needed for life's meaning and explanation.

One of the results of this secularization is the interiorization or privatization of religion. This result is now well known and well documented.[7]

Another result can be the extension of practical atheism to almost a situation of despair about this world and the direction it is taking. Fundamentalist preachers most often begin with such a jeremiad. After such a list of negatives about this world and its evils, the preacher leads up to the need for Jesus Christ and for personal conversion. Tom Sine expressed this alternative in stark terms:

> For a growing number of people in our modern world, regardless of their religious affiliation, the Creator God is no longer relevant to their lives, their society, or their future. They live in a world alienated from the God who created them — a world with no transcendent purpose, no meaning beyond the marketplace and the growing commercialization of our global society.[8]

Another reaction has been to see God's hand in working toward human liberation from all oppression. God becomes a vital force in such liberation. Unfortunately, when victory or liberation, understood in physical or economic terms, seems to be in sight, God so easily is forgotten. What had been a unifying factor during the period of oppression now is irrelevant in the post-liberation period. One senses that this attitude could so easily become dominant now in countries that had suffered much in the more recent past. I refer, for example, to countries like Poland or El Salvador. A victorious God for many in those countries is almost a contradiction in terms.

The basis for this secularization trend is clear: our scientific knowledge no longer permits us to see God as the final cause of mysterious phenomena we do not understand. We now are able to give scientific causes that are adequate and full as an explanation of natural phenomena. Where this is not so yet, we still feel that we will be able to find the answer in the near future by putting more time and money into research. The natural explanation may elude us now, but it will be found in time.

As a result of this attitude, we assume that the only matters that are of importance and that are real and accepted by all are those that we can know scientifically and can thus control. The rest that might make up the human enterprise is up to personal judgment, preference, and personal disposition.

The scientific mind also needs to find visible evidence about any phenomenon that is measurable. The healthy skepticism about this or that "miracle" now becomes a skepticism about God. We did not take seriously enough the God-is-dead theology when it was in vogue. It may have been lacking in many theological niceties, but it expressed, pushed to the extreme, a trend in our culture that was logical and predictable. For many today in their lives and in their approach to the world, God is indeed dead, not because they do not believe, but because they just do not see any signs of God in their lives and in the world around them. God is practically dead. They had been used to seeing God as the great policeman, punishing those who were doing wrong, rewarding — but most probably after this life — those who were doing good. God was the great arbiter who now is no longer needed as an explanation nor as a component of what is happening. They say that they like the newer concept of a loving God that is not out looking for ways to punish fallible humans, but they have trouble seeing how any kind of a God relates to their everyday living.

Or, what may seem at first glance somewhat contradictory, the only manifestation of God that now seems real to many is the "miracle," that is, those cases where there seems to be a suspension by God of the laws of nature that science seeks so diligently to analyze. Thus the avid pursuit after miracles and supernatural phenomena as a way of experiencing God has become almost a new and inexplicable fad in our scientific culture. The need for seeking God in the extraordinary comes when God cannot be found in the ordinary. One could say that such a search is unhealthy and often pushed by psychological needs; but it is a common phenomenon in our day, to be explained, I believe, by the absence of a need for God in our culture, because of the process of secularization that now characterizes our ordinary, daily lives.

Has belief in God become more difficult in our day because of our scientific approach to reality? I would say yes. It began before the Enlightenment but has been characteristic of our culture since then.[9] Perhaps the first sign of the divide was already evident in Francis Bacon's *Novum organum* (1620) and his distinction between *theologia naturalis* and *theologia revelata*.[10] The continual emphasis on the inductive scientific method became an integral part of our culture and has marked our civilization for several centuries. It did not lead to an atheistic and purely humanistic culture, but it left less and less space for God in our world. The bitter controversies over Genesis and the creation of the world and evolution are but one manifestation of that clash between science and faith. It is not necessary to repeat all those controversies here, but the integration of science and faith has been one of the characteristics of our period of history.[11] The result has been a purification of the concept of how God relates to this world and human history.

The peace has not always been a comfortable one and religious leaders still tend to blame science and its methods for the lack of faith in their adherents.

From this secularization process the believer is forced to give proper place to natural phenomena and their causes, while leaving the bigger picture of history in broader strokes to Divine Providence. The process of secularization has prevented thoughtful believers from declaring God's intervention in specific cases, but has not led to a loss of belief in a God who holds the key to the ultimate destiny of this earth and all on it. It has also brought a certain humility to the process and left God's hand at times shaded in mystery. It has not attempted to explain the whole of God's role in rational and human terms. It has been content finally to let God be God.

## 2. The Problem of Evil.

We know of the overpowering struggles that St. Augustine had with the concept of evil and how to reconcile that reality with a concept of a loving God.[12] In the Middle Ages that struggle never seemed to force its way into Christian consciousness again. The dualistic principle of Manichaeism no longer seemed to be an enticement to the Christian mind. It is only in our own day that this struggle has been resurrected.[13]

It is not surprising to me that the younger generation again brings up the dilemma that Augustine struggled with so earnestly. They have a deeper sense of evil in our world. The family protections are no longer present. They live in a violent world that faces them each day. The parent generation saw the nuclear arms race and lived under the continual threat of total destruction. For the first time the apocalyptic literature of the Bible as it was proclaimed in the liturgy seemed real. Although that race is now more remote, the capabilities and possibilities of total destruction remain.

The younger generation is much more influenced by violence. In addition to the media portrayal that they have become accustomed to, there is the reality of ethnic wars of extermination that do not cease. They know of the holocaust and that it happened in the memory of living people. Evil seems to triumph or dominate so often in their lives.

They are also aware of the destruction caused by drugs and sexual violence. They see the pictures of children starving in Somalia and Sudan. As a result, they have every right to ask where in such a mix the good God of revelation finds a place. It is not surprising that the old dualism of two principles, one for good and one for evil locked in a never-ending battle, appeals to them as an explanation of this world. That God only tolerates evil seems too mild and unconvincing to them as a valid explanation. It would seem more logical and more honest from their point of view just to say that this world is out of control, unguided, without rudder, helm, and helmsman.

So often one hears the younger generation say how difficult it is to believe in a God that permits children or the innocent to suffer so. How can an all-loving God permit so much evil in the world? They point out that Christianity has been around enough centuries now to make a difference. It is not enough to tell them that Christianity has not yet really been tried. They are more likely to say that it has been tried and found wanting.

I must confess that there is no good and logical explanation for this overwhelming sense of evil in the world. Vatican Council II was much more optimistic in its description of the world.[14] Some would say that we were too optimistic at that time. Such a negative and pessimistic view of the world must be balanced by a referral to the good that is also found in the world. Every priest has had to find that balance after hearing hours of confessions. People are not there to talk about the good they have done. In our world today there are many signs and evidences of good, beyond that which can be depicted in the media or sensed often from descriptions found in novels or on the screen.

Perhaps there is also some truth in the oft heard critique of the Church today that the subject of sin is not spoken of. It is an opportune moment to review the whole topic of original sin and the concept of the first Fall.[15] If the pendulum has swung too far in the direction of underestimating the existence of sin in the world, it should now be prudently brought back to the middle.

It is also helpful to do as St. Paul did and describe this battle between good and evil as found within himself and not just as a contest between outside forces in the world. That inner battle is also real and often experienced more directly by those imbued with modern culture. This explanation also can lead up to a whole new and fruitful discussion on the need for salvation, opening up a renewal of soteriology. While the theological world is preoccupied with the discussion of the uniqueness of Christ, seeking ways of reducing that position, I sense that the younger generation is searching for just the opposite, trying to find again the role of Christ as redeemer and sanctifier.[16] They are rebelling against the inherent pelagianism in American culture, seeing that it just does not work and that the spiritual dimension of the human person and in this world must also be cultivated. Out of the overwhelming weight of evil in the world is emerging the need for God's presence in a new and sustaining way.

### 3. *The Interior Experience.*

The privatization of religion has already been alluded to as characteristic of our culture. Religion was first of all excluded by Francis Bacon from the category of pure science, since it dealt with revelation and, thus, could not be subjected to scientific analysis. It was later relegated to myth or to the subjective. Since this aspect of our culture has been dealt with at such length, I do not want to make it the main focus of my attention. I only wish to assert that this tendency is real and all-pervasive and has led to a relativism that has not been helpful to religion nor to the culture itself.

Unfortunately, this aspect has been treated solely from a negative point of view in almost all literature. But to search for God within oneself was not new to the Christian ethos. The whole of the mystical or contemplative tradition was based on that assumption that God dwells within the believer and forms one of the most glorious parts of the Christian tradition. I find that it is important to keep this tradition alive and to try to absorb it into a larger picture rather than to denigrate it or to deny it. The God-within is real and very much an essential part of the Gospel message. One only has to remember the imagery of the vine and the branches to see the power behind such a realization. Intimate communion with God has been very meaningful to believers and part of the prayer tradition.

What is harmful is the limiting of God's presence to just the immanent and making one's own sentiments or emotions the criteria for God's actions. To deny this presence would, however, also be a false presentation of the Christian tradition.

The pitfalls are clear. The height of emotion cannot be the measure of the degree of presence or absence of God. That such a presence could and does result in emotional or experiential reactions should be accepted. The human person can and does have such reactions. But there remains the basic problem of relating the presence of God, spiritual as it is, to a specific degree of physical reaction. One has to be careful again of quantifying God. The literature of the mystics, however, shows that some such reaction is to be expected and accepted.

It is more difficult to explain and have accepted by the person of modern culture that, even when there is no emotional affect, God can be truly and objectively present to the person and in the person. It is at that point where the leap of faith is so important. Faith is not measured by such physical results. If the degree of emotion does not determine the quantity of God's presence, the absence of emotion does not measure it either.

The other error that can so easily follow is to make one's own experience the measure of all revealed truth. The present Pope in *Veritatis splendor* has warned against this tendency and pitfall.[17] Subjective reaction is not the basis of objective truth.

Another danger follows: privatized religion does not have of itself a communal dimension; it does not lead to community. To limit God's

influence in human affairs and history to inward
workings in each individual is to limit also the
meaning of the Incarnation. It is important to see
the same unity with God, either in the person of
Jesus Christ or of the Spirit, as a unity with others
in the same persons of the Trinity. Moving from
the subjective without denying it to the communal is not easy but must be done. If we believe that
there is also a search today for the community,
then this longing must be used to counterbalance
the first search for God's presence within. Making
that leap from the God-within to the God-within-
and-without is not impossible and should be seen
as enriching to the life of the believer. Recapturing
the communal dimension of faith should not be
done at the expense of the subjective and vice
versa.

I am sure that the privatization trend can be
used to balance the dry and rigid rubricism that so
easily creeps into religion on the hierarchical and
even liturgical level. The spread of the Charis-
matic Renewal can be seen as a way of balancing
such rigidity. It also corresponds to the desire of
our culture to be able to experience belief and not
just to hold to it in the abstract. Our culture needs
such outward manifestations if anything is to be
credible. Faith without an emotional response
would be a dead faith.

My brief observations here are a plea for both/
and, both the immanent Catholic tradition and

the communal one. I fear we will throw out the baby with the bath and miss the opportunity of renewing the finest of the mystical tradition of the faith.[18]

## 4. The Role of Authority.

There is a crisis of all authority in today's society. No institution is without its continual critics. For us citizens of the U.S.A. this critical attitude toward those in authority has been healthy and helpful. It goes back to the beginnings of the Republic and has been found in all our folk heroes. We have not accepted authority for its own sake. On the contrary, we have been skeptical and often hilariously critical of those in power.

To us in our culture there has been a demystification of authority and authority figures. We accept that the role of authority is to serve the needs of all. We expect no less. That concept of service is not far from the role of authority as described in the documents of Vatican Council II. There authority is seen also as service to all. However, the image of authority in the Church at this moment of history does not seem to correspond sufficiently to that theory.[19]

For the Church, however, the problem our culture presents is even deeper. Nothing is accepted by the scientific mind if it cannot be proven on its own merits. The real authority is the proof that comes from the experimentation itself. This

concept of science is in opposition to our concept
of revelation. For example, God reveals to us his
inner nature and workings gradually in the New
Testament for our benefit and spiritual well-being. Left to our own devices we could not arrive at
a doctrine of the Trinity. We accept such revelation on the authority of God revealing it to us. But
such a way of coming to truth is so contrary to
what the contemporary culture teaches and accepts. Faith is, thus, more difficult for the modern
mind. Since this question of authority then ex-
tends to the role of the Church, the cultural clash
intensifies. How can one believe that the Church
is the true interpreter of God's message to the
human family? The test of faith becomes more
acute.

This problem of the credibility of the Church
has been augmented in our day when so many
times its witness does not correspond to its teachings. Many then fall back on their own subjective
feelings about the faith and one ends up with a
kind of "cafeteria" Catholicism that is again a pure
subjectivism.

In the first draft of a document entitled *The
Teaching Ministry of the Diocesan Bishop* prepared
by the Committee on Doctrine of the National
Conference of Catholic Bishops the authors put
the issue succinctly:

> In summary, the bishop must teach, and teach
> authoritatively, in an intellectual culture that tends
> to reduce every religious statement to private opin-

ion and all divergencies to differences of perspec-
tives, a culture whose interests are evoked by con-
flict and whose public discourse contains challenge
and confrontation. He must teach in a world in
which popular understanding puts all authoritative
statements of the magisterium on the same level,
whether they be definitions of councils or decrees
of a Roman congregation or the teaching of an
individual bishop. Hence disagreement with any
statement of the magisterium is used to call into
question the whole fabric of authoritative teaching.
The bishop must teach in a world skeptical of
religious dogma and in the disorder native to the
open speech of a democracy.[20]

The above quote alludes to another problem
which is not well understood in the American
culture. For us, most things are either true or false
according to the validity of our scientific proof. In
the realm of theology distinctions have been made
as to the degrees of certitude — a concept almost
totally foreign to our way of thinking. Certitude
for us is certitude. But the Church has added
"theological notes" to its basic teaching, because
some is of absolute Divine revelation and other is
of theological opinion. These distinctions have
been lost in our modern teaching methods and I
believe the result has been inimical to the whole
question of authority itself.

One also has to reckon with the way in which
the mass media today teaches in its own right.
Whenever a scholar produces a new idea, that idea
immediately finds its way into the mass media.
Formerly such newer concepts were tested in

scientific periodicals that were not available to the person on the street. Now the believers are subjected to every new idea at once and before it has been tested by other scholars and other authority figures in religion. So often, too, the new concept has not been tested for its pastoral implications.

One would have to add also that the large number of scandals in so many religious groups today, including the Catholic Church, have lessened the weight of authority and its ability to function. This lack of credibility will turn out to be one of the major problems that all Churches must face in the near future.

One also hears today that there are other kinds of authority besides those which are part of the hierarchical structure of the Church. Theologians have their own authority which is intrinsic to their field. That authority should not be neglected, because it comes from years of reflection and investigation. Because these authorities often clash in today's culture, the believer becomes either confused or simply relegates the whole question of theological dispute to a minor level.

One aspect of the whole question of authority that has not been thoroughly investigated in our day is the question of the "sensus fidelium." Scholars of the last century, especially Cardinal Newman, spoke much of this role of the faithful.[21] An analysis of this concept involves the whole concept of receptivity on the part of the faithful of the teaching authority. This delicate issue should not be neglected. So many incidences in history can be produced which show how important receptivity has been for the ongoing well-being of the Church itself. Naturally, the fear on the part of authority is that this criterion of receptivity could easily reduce the Church to a democratic process in which the majority vote of the people would determine truth. Such a conclusion would be just as wrong and just as contrary to our scientific mentality as saying that any one individual alone possesses all truth. It would seem that the future will demand a greater clarification of the role of the "sensus fidelium" and how it interacts with Church teaching. If the danger on one side is that of a total democratization of the Church that could lead to a majority rule in the determination of truth, the fear on the other side is that of a creeping infallibility which goes beyond its mandate and seems to smother all contrary and contributing voices.

Pastorally it is important to present the Church's teaching clearly to the young with the degree of certitude that each teaching enjoys. Such a process should not lead, however, to a rapid dismissal of a teaching when there seems to be a clear disagreement with the culture. So often the culture does indeed need critiquing and it is the role of the Church in proclaiming the Gospel to provide precisely that kind of challenge. Today I would say that most people weigh down too heavily without reflection against the Church and in favor of the culture, when so often it is the culture that truly needs critiquing.

It is important also for the Church today to recapture its role as an instrument of salvation. That God can work through people, signs and symbols, is a part of the Church's tradition that needs a revitalization. The sacramental principle that has been a part of our heritage from earliest patristic times is one of the chief ways in which we see God relating to this world. That role of the Church as an instrument of salvation and a sacrament to the world needs further elucidation if it is to become a part of popular Catholic culture again. God reaches out in ways that are truly human and available to all. The principle of sacramentality is also a principle of how the Incarnation, that is, God's presence among us, continues down through the ages through the action of the Holy Spirit. Perhaps at this point of history we have placed so much emphasis on the Church as teacher and on the Church's teaching role that we have missed the basic attitude that must be there of seeing the Church as sacrament. In recapturing that role other aspects of authority will fall into place.

It is not easy for people today, however, to accept sacraments as truly encounters with Christ. We need a revitalization of the whole question of

the Paschal Mystery, of the Death and Resurrection of the Lord, and how that historical event
reaches us in the 20th century. More basically,
perhaps what also is missing in our culture is a
deep historical sense. Although this has been said
often of U.S. culture in particular, I find that such
a lack is disappearing and that Americans are
indeed becoming a historical people.

The question of sacraments and instrumen-
tality and the awareness of mediated grace is one
of the many concepts our present generation finds
difficulty with, because God's action in these areas
cannot be placed under a microscope and measured. It is true that they do demand an enormous
amount of faith. I would have to be honest and say
that I am not at all a promulgator of the ideas that
some attribute to Karl Rahner that the sacraments
only celebrate that which is already present in
nature. It seems to me that this is not a traditional
Catholic viewpoint and reduces God and sacraments in a way that is untraditional. I have seen in
pastoral practice that it leads to a total disregard
for the importance of sacraments. It strikes me
that one has to return in some measure to a more
objective stance if God's free action is to be
appreciated.

In the decades to come perhaps no other area
will see the cultural clash as significantly as this
area of authority. It must be worked on, however,
rationally and calmly.

## 5. *The Aesthetic Void*

Those who study religion have always been fascinated by the relationship between the aesthetic experience and the religious experience. It has almost always been presupposed that such a relationship exists. In Christian terms this relationship has often been the object of a struggle. At various times in the history of the Church the fear has arisen that the religious experience could be subsumed under the aesthetic and not, as it were, be the dominant one. That fear goes back to the early Church where most of the converts from paganism or from Hellenistic cults wanted to reject the aesthetic experiences of the previous life and not carry them over into the Church. One sees similar phenomena today in missionary lands where the aesthetic experiences of the past are not helpful for the process of inculturation.

For this reason, the early Church tended to be anti-aesthetic. One would say that this hesitation was more in the writings about worship than in the actual performance of the liturgy, because one senses almost immediately a carry-over of aesthetic refinement into the early Church worship.

In the history of the Catholic Church, however, there has always been a close relationship between the aesthetic experience and the religious one. The monastic tradition, beginning with St. Basil and very clearly enunciated by St. Benedict, reveals that religious current as advocating the importance of that aesthetic experience. Benedict does not permit everyone to read and sing in church but only those who could do so well. He permits only those who could "edify the listeners" to be a part of the public reading and singing.[22] Because of that monastic position there arose the whole beauty of Gregorian Chant and the splendid monastic architecture. Benedict seemed aware of the fact that music and space influenced the human spirit and one's ability to commune with God.

The battle was not won, however, so easily, as we see in the lives of both Augustine and Jerome. One could say that Augustine struggled most with this question, always fearful that he was making the aesthetic experience equivalent to the religious. He saw this as a temptation, but, nevertheless, continued to admire the aesthetic. One could say that he learned to use the aesthetic as a springboard for faith and not as an equivalent thereof. In doing so he established the great religious tradition that the aesthetic experience can be a sign or symbol that assists in the act of faith. The Columban Irish monks adhered more to the tradition of St. Jerome. Bernard was also aware of this negative attitude and struggled with it.

In the Middle Ages the position of Augustine was taken for granted as art, architecture, and music evolved. The Gothic architecture was indeed a religious experience. One sees that same experience in all the didactic material that was used to teach the faithful about the Bible and the Christian faith. Not only the architecture but all of the sculpture and art are clearly indicative of triumph of the aesthetic in this didactic approach. Beauty is just taken for granted and helps the believer be drawn in to the numinous, the mysterious, and awe-full presence of God.

One could also say that this same general attitude, although applied in a very different way, characterized the Church during the period of the Renaissance. The challenges of the new concepts of beauty, especially of the human body, were accepted by all artists, the Italians in particular. They attempted to portray the body in a very vivid way also within a spiritual and religious context. One could say that the revival of Greek models did not do harm to the religious sentiment even though it did present challenges and struggles. Here, too, the aesthetic was used as a springboard for the religious experience.

In baroque times that challenge was modified somewhat and an evident split between secular and sacred became evident in both theory and practice. That split in mentality has remained with us to the present day. It varied in various sections of Europe but has never been totally overcome.

If one were writing on the subject of seeking God in the last century, there is no doubt that the aesthetic experience would have been very much highlighted as a part of the whole Catholic tradition. It would have been seen as a way in which God reaches the human person. In that period, one sees the revival of Gothic architecture, the renewal of Gregorian Chant, and the whole fascination with the medieval as the epitome of how one can reach God through the aesthetic. So many of the converts to Catholicism took that route in the last century. Those who left the faith and returned or even those who were only marginally attached to the Church recognized the allurement of the aesthetic experience within the Church. One can think, for example, of Franz Liszt and those who surrounded him. Perhaps no other person outlined this allurement in an apologetic way better than Chateaubriand in his *Génie du Christianisme.*[23] In that famous work Chateaubriand outlined the importance of the aesthetic in the whole history of Catholicism and used it as a proof for the presence of God within the Church.

Our own present day culture has seen almost a total breakdown between religion and the arts. It would seem that our culture has found difficulty in expressing the religious in a convincing way through its cultural media. Such a gap has definitely affected Catholic worship and Catholic life. One could say without equivocation that the most famous contemporary composers of music in particular have not written for the Church. This cannot be said, however, of architecture which has had a more positive history. It has flourished in more recent decades, especially since Vatican II. Original Church architecture has been the object of much interest and creative activity on the part of architects.

There is today a cultural and artistic void that has not been helpful for the expression of religious sentiment. In music in particular that void has been felt. In this post-Vatican II period the revival of Gregorian Chant has not solved the problem. Older music that stemmed from the earliest attempts of vernacular liturgies in the 16th and 17th century has been helpful. It has been a part of most of the Protestant traditions and now borrowed again into Catholicism. I would say that Catholics in general sense this loss and feel helpless with regard to it.

One could say that the Catholic tradition has always maintained that there was a relationship between that aesthetic experience and a sense of the transcendent and majestic. The loss of that aesthetic quality has tended in the minds of most to make religion almost purely horizontal, as it were, and has provoked a loss of the vertical.

One of the unfortunate results of the liturgical reforms of Vatican Council II has been a leveling of taste so that one could say that the tastes of mass culture have entered the Church. They cannot compete with the more ennobling and didactic

models of the past. The Church has always recognized that there is also a didactic quality to art and
that it can and does ennoble people and inspire
them to greater virtue. That tradition has been
lost.

The cultural void and the reduction of taste to
the least common denominator has not been
helpful in the search for God today. One could
almost say that the aesthetic experience no longer
is found in the churches and no longer, thus, can
edify as Benedict desired. One even hears of such
monstrosities as "Polka Masses" which take people
in a most offensive way away from a sense of God's
presence into the ballroom and onto the dance
floor.

The renewal of Church music, art, and architecture is an absolute must in the quest for God in
our present day. First-rate composers writing music
that will last, religious sculpture, paintings, and
buildings that are more than functional — such a
renewal has not been totally realized.

However, one does not have to be totally
negative. Perhaps we ask too much of church
buildings and liturgy. People still have deep aesthetic experiences outside of Church that lead to
a deeper awakening of the presence of God in their
lives and in the world. So, for example, many who
see some of the wonders of nature are still overcome by a sense of God's presence there. Music
and art that is not totally and rigidly religious can

still be the cause of an aesthetic experience that leads one to make the faith leap. One could almost say that today the aesthetic void in Church has led people, because of a deep need within the human person, to aesthetic religious experiences outside Church.

Sometimes, because of the lack of the aesthetic aids that were there in the past, people in this search for God in our day have tended to reduce worship to a kind of comradery or good feeling toward other human beings. Rather than the aesthetic experience becoming then the platform for the faith leap, good will and feeling of community have substituted for it.

There is no doubt that this issue, namely, the need for the aesthetic experience, can vary greatly from person to person in our own cultural pluralism today. For this reason it is not always easy to find the kind of an answer that is helpful to the majority. Personally, I still feel that the Church in its best tradition has leaned toward a kind of "elitism" in this aesthetic realm, seeing how banal and crass liturgical worship can become if it does not do so. Perhaps even a grain of that elitism might balance some of the weaknesses now evident in Church worship.

## 6. Patriarchal Images

In the search for God in our own day there has been a very natural tendency to ask questions about the way in which God has been historically presented in our Catholic faith. The patriarchal roots are most evident and cannot be denied. The image of God that is present in the Old Testament and that continues into the New Testament is indeed highly masculine and patriarchal. For some in our day that has been a decided impediment in the quest for the presence of God in their lives and is seen as far too limited.

I need not talk at great length about this trend to broaden the images of God in our culture today and how important it is. One only has to look at the catalogue of recently published books, especially doctoral dissertations, to see how much has been written on that subject.[24] Many would say that it has become almost an obsession and has brought about a new imbalance that almost denies the previous tradition and literature.

God-talk today is not easy because of these sensitivities. There is indeed a need for balance. Without going into great detail on this very intricate argument and citing the enormous literature that is present, I believe I could sum up my own position by saying that there has been an enrichment in our concept of God and quest for God by the introduction of the more feminine aspects of the deity. This attempt to balance the patriarchal imagery has been a good one. On the other hand, there is also the tendency to deny the tradition; and such an extreme swing cannot be helpful but will create a new imbalance. Molding together all of the good from tradition as well as present insights and creating a synthesis that will be well articulated and balanced is perhaps one of the greatest challenges we have today in our God-search.

On the other hand, I must confess that at this point I do not see how we can find new language for the Trinity and the processions in the Trinity that maintains the fullness of our tradition. That tradition has been expressed in male terms and it is not quite clear how that will be redressed.

All agree that God is indeed without gender; but we do not have linguistic terms that can portray the vitality of a person if that person is presented as genderless. The result could be a kind of neutralizing that would not be helpful in the quest for God.

I do not intend to go into great detail on this issue but certainly want to point it out as important for the search for God in our day and an area that is vital to almost every Christian. Balance as well as creativity are both needed at this point of history, so that there can be a vital link between all of the literature that is being produced on this subject and the pastoral needs of our people. How theology can be turned into spiritual growth is not always clear.

*Epilogue*

I would now like to sum up some of the aspects of the search for God in our contemporary culture that strike me as being most important. These aspects do not deny the need for faith, but show rather how that faith can be supported and at times enlarged through the culture in which we live.

1. Walter Kasper many years ago wrote, "If the word 'God' is to have any meaning at all, it must assert a 'something' which is not identical with humanity, the world, and history."[25] There is a need in our contemporary culture to emphasize this "otherness" aspect of God. Only in that way can we balance some of the immanentism that is so much a part of the privatization of religion. We must realize that God is indeed with us, but never totally possessed by us. There is a God beyond us that is independent of us and drags us forward to a higher destiny. That larger view of God that is often equated with terms like "awe" or the *mysterium tremendum* must be again emphasized. The Catholic tradition has always been a both/and tradition and, therefore, it is important to supply the balance where there are *lacunae* in our transmission of the heritage that has been ours. One should not think that our own culture is not helpful in this regard. There is certainly a quest among people for meaning that goes beyond their own experience and their own knowledge. They

realize the limitations of human knowledge and
the need to find a more ultimate explanation. It is
interesting that modern physics has been an aid in
this search and certainly not a hindrance. Years
ago one could have talked about science as a
substitute for religion, but that today would make
no sense. Our culture is ripe now for a deeper and
more spiritual and transcendent approach.

2. There is need to accept as valid the interior
experiences of the human person with regard to
God's presence. One should not deny that interi-
ority because of some of the dangers that may be
involved. In that same regard one has to increase
the aesthetic value of experience and its possibility
to be a springboard for the faith leap. The
interiorization of religion should not be taken as
the equivalent of privatization. Interiorization can
also mean sharing in the larger vision of a God who
acts also outside the individual human person.

3. In outlining that larger vision of God's
Providence, there is no doubt that a deep faith is
required. God's ultimate presence in the history of
the human race and this world must not be seen
only in the here and now. A revitalization of the
whole eschatological thrust of Christianity is
needed if God's presence in the here and now is to
make sense. God possesses an ultimate destiny and
plan for this world and that plan will not be
thwarted. If one accepts that larger destiny for the
world and the people on it, then our own inner
position becomes clearer.

4. It is important that faith help us to experience the reality of this world in a new and different way. We must recapture the Incarnational principle that God entered human history to give it a new and higher meaning. Through the death and resurrection of Jesus Christ and the sending of the Spirit, all reality has taken on a new dimension that one could call "sacramental." Sometimes that sacramental dimension is not immediately visible. It involves a tremendous struggle with evil, but the ultimate victory through the resurrection is a part of the faith and hope that is the mainstay of every believer.

To experience reality in that different way under faith means to give meaning and significance to all of life and to what happens in this world. Perhaps God will be found less now in the natural disasters than in the past; but God's Providence can indeed be found in the love, the joy, the friendship, and the trust of others. All these other aspects make human relationships special places for the search of God's presence. It may well be that in our day we have passed from seeing God in nature to seeing God in people. Human relationships that are based on love and fidelity, trust and mutuality, become places where God's presence can be both discovered and somehow experienced.

Only in this way will life take on new meaning and God's presence in our midst be significant. In a sense, one then finds the mysterious not in an abstract God, but one finds the mysterious presence of God in human relationships as they share in the mystery of the Godhead and its own inner dynamics.

5. Discovering new meaning for this world through God's presence in it also entails finding new purpose in suffering and in some of those aspects of life that seem to be negative and even evil. One cannot ignore these very real negative aspects of human life. For this reason it would be important to make sure that suffering becomes meaningful. Such a realization brings new life and vitality to the whole Paschal Mystery of the suffering and death of Christ. Making suffering meaningful and redemptive must be a part of the Christian vision of God operating and acting in our midst. Such an attitude has deep pastoral implications. I have found recently that a return to the old theology of "offering it up" is not without deep meaning for people who are suffering. It gives meaning and makes sense to them in a way often that is not articulated but indeed quite real.

St. Benedict knew that the quest for God would never end. As mentioned earlier, he does not expect the novice to find God, but only to continue the search. It is well for us to remember his admonition at this moment of history with regard to our present culture. There are many negative aspects of that culture that are a hindrance in the search for God, but I sense that there are enough positive aspects to make that search both meaningful and exciting. The search makes no sense, of course, if one does not have a strong belief in God. On the other hand, the search increases the solidity of the belief and one continually marvels at the enrichment that comes from such a quest under the power of a deep faith and belief.

It is to be presupposed that, when many people seek God in our culture and give a deeper spiritual meaning to the reality in which they live and the culture that surrounds it, that culture itself will begin to change. One would only hope that the culture then would become a clearer vehicle for religious expression than it is at this present moment. The fault must be found, however, not in the culture but in those who have failed to express their deep religious sentiments in and through the better aspects of the culture that are able to carry a sense of the transcendent. The quest will continue only if we put all of our strength and energy into it. True merit, though, does not come from finding, but from seeking.

*Notes*

1. Pertinent literature on this word and the criteria can be found in: Timothy Fry, O.S.B., ed., *The Rule of St. Benedict* (Collegeville, MN: Liturgical Press, 1981), 447-48.

2. One of the main characteristics of the pontificate of Pope John Paul II has been his constant concern with the relationship between culture and faith. Some of the most exciting and engaging theology of our day has come out of the reflection on this relationship between revelation and culture. One could cite, for example, at once the works of David Tracy, beginning with his *Blessed Rage for Order* (New York: Seabury, 1975) and his subsequent works. See also his more recent: "The Uneasy Alliance Reconceived: Catholic Theological Method, Modernity, and Postmodernity," *Theological Studies* 50 (September 1989): 548-70. All of liberation theology could also be listed under such a heading. Michael Buckley wrote on this subject in a seminal essay on contemporary atheism: "If the judgment of Rahner is correct that the efforts of the Church to deal with the contemporary situation have been ineffectual, may part of this not lie with the isolation of theology from a prolonged and disciplined attempt to mediate between religion and contemporary culture and to formulate the inherent problems correctly?" *Theological Studies* 50 (September 1989): 461.

3. See the classic work on this question: H. Richard Niebuhr, *Christ and Culture* (New York: Harper & Row, 1951).

4. When Harvey Cox published his book, *The Secular City* (New York: Macmillan, 1965), it soon became the classic for reflection on the trend toward "Death of God" theology and secularization. The mid-1960s saw many books on this same theme, all hotly debated in theological circles: Paul van Buren, *The Secular Meaning of the Gospel* (New York: Macmillan, 1963); Thomas Altizer and William Hamilton, *Radical Theology and the Death of God* (Indianapolis: Bobbs-Merrill, 1966); Thomas J.J. Altizer, *The Gospel of Christian Atheism* (Philadelphia: Westminster Press, 1970).

5. The most often cited text in this regard is from *Gaudium et spes,* #36: "Many of our contemporaries, however, seem to fear that a closer connection between human activity and religion will prejudice the autonomy of humanity, of societies or of the sciences. If we take the autonomy of earthly realities to mean that created things, and societies also, have their own laws and values which are to be gradually discovered, utilised and ordered by us, then it is perfectly proper to claim such autonomy as not only demanded by people today but as in harmony with the will of the creator. From the fact of being created, every thing possesses its own stability, truth and goodness, and its own laws and order, which should be respected by us in recognising the methods which are appropriate to the various sciences and arts." I have used the translation from Norman P. Tanner, S.J., ed., *Decrees of the Ecumenical Council* (Washington DC: Georgetown University Press, 1990), Vol. II, 1090.

6. Andrew Greeley, *Unsecular Man* (New York: Delta, 1972). The works of Greeley still stand as the

best analysis of contemporary religious culture that we have in the U.S.A. It is to be noted that Tracy in his second major work, *The Analogical Imagination: Christian Theology and the Culture of Pluralism* (New York: Crossroad 1981), p. 87, n. 43, accepted the modifications presented by Greeley to the secularization debate. It seemed strange to me that Harvey Cox did not mention the work of Greeley in his subsequent book, *Religion in the Secular City: Toward a Postmodern Theology* (New York: Simon & Schuster, 1984).

7. Robert N. Bellah, Richard Madsen, William M. Sullivan, Ann Swidler, and Steven M. Tipton, *Habits of the Heart: Individualism and Commitment in American Life* (Berkeley: University of California Press, 1985); *Individualism and Commitment in American Life : Readings on the Themes of "Habits of the Heart"* (New York: Harper & Row, 1987); and *The Good Society* (New York: Alfred A. Knopf, 1991).

8. Tom Sine, *Wild Hope* (Dallas: Word Publishing, 1991), 215.

9. See an allusion to this phenomenon in the Renaissance in Richard Marius, *Thomas More* (New York: Random House, 1985). He states: "I think it [the religious revolution of the sixteenth century] arose partly out of a profound skepticism about Christianity itself and that many people who battled and burned each other over dogma were fighting away a horrendous doubt that God ruled in His creation" (p. X). For this essay and for the historical part in particular I found the neglected work of Bernard J. Cooke, *The Distancing of God: The Ambiguity of Symbol in History and Theology* (Minneapolis: Fortress Press, 1990), of special help.

10. F. H. Anderson, *The Philosophy of Francis Bacon* (Chicago: University of Chicago Press, 1948), 298.

11. See Stanley L. Jaki, *The Road of Science and the Ways to God* (Edinburgh: Scottish Academic Press, 1978) and Langdon Gilkey, *Religion and the Scientific Future: Reflections on Myth, Science, and Theology* (New York: Harper & Row, 1970).

12. Peter Brown, *Augustine of Hippo* (Berkeley: University of California Press, 1967) 46-48, 148-50.

13. Paul Ricoeur, *The Symbolism of Evil,* trans. by Emerson Buchanan (New York: Harper & Row, 1967).

14. If one reads carefully *Gaudium et spes,* one finds that it is not such an optimistic document as such. It points out many of the problems of the contemporary culture. What is positive is the sense that one can do something about the evils that exist. There was at that time an optimism about change that is not present now.

15. *Reconciliation and Penance* (Washington, DC: USCC Publications, 1984). The Synod of Bishops had struggled with these concepts in an attempt to articulate them in modern terms and still remain true to the tradition of the Church.

16. It is difficult to keep up with the enormous literature in this field about the uniqueness of Jesus Christ. See, in particular, the works of Paul Knitter. His most known work in this area is: *No Other Name? A Critical Survey of Christian Attitudes Toward World Religions* (Maryknoll: Orbis Books, 1985).

17. *Veritatis splendor,* #63.

18. In modern times it was Friedrich von Hügel who emphasized the mystical quality, together with the

institutional and intellectual, as characteristic of all great religions. See: *The Mystical Element in Religion* (2 vols.: New York: Dutton, 1923).

19. Two classics in this field are: John L. McKenzie, *Authority in the Church* (New York: Sheed & Ward, 1966), and Raymond Edward Brown, *Priest and Bishop: Biblical Reflections* (Paramus, NJ: Paulist Press, 1970). It is to be noted that both books come out of recent biblical studies, especially on authority in the New Testament.

20. National Conference of Catholic Bishops, Committee on Doctrine, May 1991, p. 6.

21. See the edition of John Henry Newman's *On Consulting the Faithful in Matters of Doctrine* (Kansas City, MO: Sheed & Ward, 1961), with a lengthy and helpful introduction by John Coulson.

22. Twice Benedict brings up this idea that the readers or singers should edify the listeners; see chapter 38, 12 and chapter 47, 3.

23. François Auguste René Chateaubriand, *Génie du Christianisme* (Tournai: Casterman, 1843). I confess to having read the *Génie du Christianisme* in an English translation called *The Genius of Christianity: or The Spirit and Beauty of the Christian Religion* (Baltimore: J. Murphy Co., 1856) during my first year in college and to the profound effect it had upon me at that time.

24. The most thoughtful work in this quest is undoubtedly that by Elizabeth A. Johnson, *She who is: The Mystery of God in Feminist Theological Discourse* (New York: Crossroad, 1992). See the many works she cites in that study.

25. See the article "How can we experience God today," *Theology Digest* 18 (Summer 1970) p. 123. This is a résumé of his important article "Möglichkeiten der Gotteserfahrung heute," *Geist und Leben,* 42 (1969), 329-49. He has elaborated on these themes in his extensive study, *The God of Jesus Christ,* trans. by Matthew J. O'Connell (New York: Crossroad, 1984), especially in Part I, "The God-Question Today."

# THE PÈRE MARQUETTE LECTURES IN THEOLOGY

1969 *The Authority for Authority*
        Quentin Quesnell
        Professor of Theology
        Marquette University

1970 *Mystery and Truth*
        John Macquarrie
        Professor of Theology
        Union Theological Seminary

1971 *Doctrinal Pluralism*
        Bernard Lonergan, S.J.
        Professor of Theology
        Regis College, Ontario

1972 *Infallibility*
        George A. Lindbeck
        Professor of Theology
        Yale University

1973 *Ambiguity in Moral Choice*
        Richard A. McCormick, S.J.
        Professor of Moral Theology
        Bellarmine School of Theology

1974 *Church Membership as a Catholic and Ecumenical Problem*
        Avery Dulles, S.J.
        Professor of Theology
        Woodstock College

1975 *The Contributions of Theology to Medical Ethics*
James Gustafson
University Professor of Theological Ethics
University of Chicago

1976 *Religious Values in an Age of Violence*
Rabbi Marc Tannenbaum
Director of National Interreligious Affairs
American Jewish Committee, New York City

1977 *Truth Beyond Relativism:*
*Karl Mannheim's Sociology of Knowledge*
Gregory Baum
Professor of Theology and Religious Studies
St. Michael's College

1978 *A Theology of 'Uncreated Energies'*
George A. Maloney, S.J.
Professor of Theology
John XXIII Center for Eastern Christian
Studies
Fordham University

1980 *Method in Theology:*
*An Organon For Our Time*
Frederick E. Crowe, S.J.
Research Professor in Theology
Regis College, Toronto

1981 *Catholics in the Promised Land of the Saints*
James Hennesey, S.J.
Professor of the History of Christianity
Boston College

1982 *Whose Experience Counts in Theological Reflection?*
Monika Hellwig
Professor of Theology
Georgetown University

1983 *The Theology and Setting of Discipleship in the Gospel of Mark*
John R. Donahue, S.J.
Professor of Theology
Jesuit School of Theology, Berkeley

1984 *Should War be Eliminated? Philosophical and Theological Investigations*
Stanley Hauerwas
Professor of Theology
Notre Dame University

1985 *From Vision to Legislation: From the Council to a Code of Laws*
Ladislas M. Orsy, S.J.
Professor of Canon Law
The Catholic University of America

1986 *Revelation and Violence: A Study in Contextualization*
Walter Brueggemann
Professor of Old Testament
Eden Theological Seminary
St. Louis, Missouri

Marquette University

1987 *Nova et Vetera:*
   *The Theology of Tradition in American Catholicism*
      Gerald Fogarty
      Professor of Religious Studies
      University of Virginia

1988 *The Christian Understanding of Freedom and the*
   *History of Freedom in the Modern Era:*
   *The Meeting and Confrontation Between*
   *Christianity and the Modern Era in a Postmodern*
   *Situation*
      Walter Kasper
      Professor of Dogmatic Theology
      University of Tübingen

1989 *Moral Absolutes: Catholic Tradition, Current*
   *Trends, and the Truth*
      William F. May
      Ordinary Professor of Moral Theology
      Catholic University of America

1990 *Is Mark's Gospel a Life of Jesus? The Question of*
   *Genre*
      Adela Yarbro Collins
      Professor of New Testament
      University of Notre Dame

1991 *Faith, History and Cultures:*
   *Stability and Change in Church Teachings*
      Walter H. Principe, C.S.B.
      Professor of Theology
      University of Toronto

THE PÈRE MARQUETTE LECTURES IN THEOLOGY

Uniform format, cover, and binding.
Copies of this Lecture and the others in the series are
obtainable from:

Marquette University Press
Marquette University
Milwaukee WI 53233 U.S.A.

(414) 288 1564   ***   (414) 288-3300 (fax)
University and Book Store Purchase Orders. Visa, MasterCard,
Discover, American Express.